T0304533

WHEN THE TIME COMES

poems

HANK LAZER

DOS MADRES

2022

DOS MADRES PRESS INC.

P.O. Box 294, Loveland, Ohio 45140

www.dosmadres.com   editor@dosmadres.com

Dos Madres is dedicated to the belief that the small press is essential to the vitality of contemporary literature as a carrier of the new voice, as well as the older, sometimes forgotten voices of the past. And in an ever more virtual world, to the creation of fine books pleasing to the eye and hand.

Dos Madres is named in honor of Vera Murphy and Libbie Hughes, the "Dos Madres" whose contributions have made this press possible.

Dos Madres Press, Inc. is an Ohio Not For Profit Corporation and a 501 (c) (3) qualified public charity. Contributions are tax deductible.

Executive Editor: Robert J. Murphy

Illustration & Book Design: Elizabeth H. Murphy
www.illusionstudios.net

Cover Photo: Hank Lazer

Typeset in Adobe Garamond Pro & Goudy Old Style
ISBN 978-1-953252-51-7
Library of Congress Control Number: 2022930832

ACKNOWLEDGEMENTS

This did not seem to me to be a book that would have benefited from taking out individual poems or sections to send to magazines. So, no magazine publications.

Instead, I acknowledge friends and family who read the poems and helped me to believe in their value – to them, to myself, to my family, to other readers. Thanks to Joseph Lease, Donna de la Perrière, Glenn Mott, Charles Bernstein, Norman Fischer, Linda Goodman, and Ben Poe. Thanks too, indirectly, to Joan Halifax whose book *Being with Dying* provides wisdom and instruction in this difficult and treasured practice of turning toward rather than away from the dying of a loved one. Thanks, too, for the examples of the late poems of Robert Creeley, Wallace Stevens, and William Carlos Williams – by my side during those final weeks.

Special thanks to my sister, Terri, for being with me and my mother during these final weeks. Thanks to my step-father, Jerry Bookin, for his loving and devoted care for my mother. And thanks to my mother's two closest care providers, Gail Caporaletti and Illa Santa Monica.

It takes a village to raise a child. It takes a village – of friends, family, poets, publishers – to make such a book. Thanks, Robert & Elizabeth Murphy.

WHEN THE TIME COMES

how lovely is the book
        product of quiet mornings
                product of yes no & maybe

how lovely is the book
        extending hours of grief
                providing clothing for memory

how lovely is the book
        immersed in sorrow & injustice
                refusing all false hope

how lovely is the book
        product of many hands
                community of gathered words

how lovely is the book
        attending to the sound of each syllable
                with its secret music

how lovely is the book
        seeing clearly
                having given up all ideas

how lovely is the book
        uncertain of itself
                until you take it up

how lovely is the book
        which you have chosen
                & which has chosen you

In memory of my mother,
Wendy Lazer
(August 18, 1930 – April 30, 2021)

the death of
one is
many

—Robert Creeley,
  A Day Book

To die is our virtue;
to come into this world
is also our virtue.

—Shunryu Suzuki,
  Branching Streams Flow in the Darkness

Deathwatch for my Mother, Wendy Lazer

(April 14-21, 2021)

there it was   4/14/2021
&   that is that
a life come down
to amazingly loud

screams   yelling
for *mommy & daddy*
i want to go home
help   help

last resort last
stop on the line
morphine   every hour
alternating terror & rest

where is the home
you want to go to i ask
& you say with such
pain   *i don't know*

& you say you have seen
an angel in the room
do you know the angel's name
in pain you say   *i don't know*

& the angel does not
bring comfort or peace
when the door is open
the entire hall can hear your screams

each day the same
until it isn't
& after that
what is there

that changes
perhaps not
for you
but for us

in adjustments
& surprises of memory
as we find our way
into your state

you grow intimate
with death
which your screams
never address

you are given more   4/15/2021
oxygen   small amounts
of liquids in a teaspoon
this morning very early

i am writing your
obituary   words are not
candles   there is
no capturing of

a life   not yours
not mine   not
anyone's   impossible
to live this life

yet we do it day
by day   i listen
but do not know
the screaming final

space that you
occupy   a list
of what you've done
& where you've been

doesn't touch the twisted
bitter & brilliant
intelligence of your life
tops in your high school

class way back in mythic
brooklyn   instead of cornell
your parents told you
they were saving their money

for your younger brother
he became a neurosurgeon
& you left brooklyn for
california to live a life

equally brilliant
pianist   mother
business woman
always successful

always driven
a passion for
symphony   opera   painting
& exaggeration

every thing better
or best   pleading for
your parents' love & approval
long after they were dead

funny that as you
are dying you
call out to them
strange   because

as jews we do not
believe in a place
where you will see them
again   perhaps then

a call for them
to embrace &
recognize the beautiful
jewish accomplishment of your life

turn the page & it's
about what to do with
clothing   shoes   handbags
& jewelry   & then

the ashes   already in
forethought scattered
on oahu   in pebble beach
in san josé   in alabama

ashes ashes all
fall down   we each
move up a notch
toward that inevitable hospital bed

you said it was
the weather &
the people   the best
air on earth

always ready with ad copy
for wherever you lived
& whatever you bought
fact is you live

on an island
which is the farthest
place on earth
from anything else

when it is said
peace
which surpasseth
understanding

it does ring true
here to there
here to where
what exactly

is happening
as you become
memory   invisible
& yet so present

each life is the same life
a struggle with pain
suffering loss & disappointment
with momentary glimpses

of something else
to live by vow
is a difficult way
what is the most

important thing
to find that out
as suzuki roshi says
is the most important thing

not at peace with
dying   death will
take you any way
for us there is

no resurrection
nothing
next
right or wrong

it is not a
rehearsal
this life is lived
right here

too conscious of too many   WS/271   4/17/2021
things at once   in your light   WS/285
the head is speaking
in your light   or dark

which we will visit soon
early morning   & you will
awaken to mysteriously compelled
yelling   familiar voices   &

a fading love moving into
transition   this music
a cable soundscape   too generic
to have specific meaning

the sun is old & mostly
absent   somewhere outside
it really is spring   you
& your yelling spiral downward

into silence   what is a
breath   taken one at a
time   find it   soon *hurry*
you will find it

my sister & i   come to be
with you   greet the dawn
with coffee on the balcony
for us   a slow succession of days

your husband   your daughter
your son   each coping
as you are   in an individual
& inward way with your dying

i do not feel whole
without these words
knowing though they are
to you of little use

eyes & shadows   ears
alert & acute   who knows
what is happening
in your scrolling mind

we are with your paintings
& your music   artificial
orchids   & way too many
coffee cups   a home

fit to your specifications
now empty of you
weeks now in a single
bed   in another building

description less important
than the event
when the boulder
rolls down the hill

whoever says malice
does not understand
this simply   this is
what happens

whenever it does
between one breath
& the next
a thin bookmark

or a feather
placed between the pages
of a closed & still
treasured book

beside the children's quiet
field of play   small birds
disappear into the carefully
trimmed crown of a tree

everywhere   on this island &
everywhere   density
of human presence &
invisible death of

everything else we
displace with steady pleasure
mostly oblivious to
this consequential manifest destiny

gown gloves face shield   4/18/2021
& mask   we enter
your room   morphine
klonopin   & another new

anti-psychotic barely touch
you   every five seconds
you croak out a steady
syllable   *ma   ma   ma*

sometimes *help* sometimes
out   my sister & i
encounter a black box
no way to know

what is going on inside
no way to know if
the shouted syllable
carries any meaning

we are told it is a rare
neurological response
perhaps the result of
brain cancer   you do

answer some questions   are you
in pain   NO   do you know
we are here   YES   then
the return of MA MA MA

this morning a wonderful
sunrise over the mountain ridge
nearly blind   & the window
in your room faces the opposite

way   a sunrise you cannot see
john cage was fond of saying
every day is a beautiful day
is it?   i ask neither for

nor against the proposition
you are still breathing & we
still can visit you & listen
to your agitated repetition

of that one fundamental
syllable   *ma   ma   ma*
as if it were a koan
or perhaps a glitch within

your brain so that no matter
what you might wish to
say only this syllable
comes out   *ma   ma   ma*

if we give it meaning
then it becomes something
but my sister & i know
that you felt betrayed &

unappreciated by your mother so
at age 18 you left brooklyn
to get away from your parents
gone to california to stay with

your aunt sonia   gone
from brooklyn for good
soon to marry & start
your own family far

away from *ma* who
eventually made her
own way to san josé
to be with you & her

sister & brothers
so my sister & i
figure that the call
ma   ma   ma   has

little to do with
some hoped for reunion
your cry   *ma   ma   ma*
is like the waving figure

on the shore seen from
the sea in crane's "open boat"
the waving is not a rescue
& we must conclude

the gesture has no meaning
or when suzuki roshi was
asked "why is there so much
suffering?" he answered: "no reason"

this morning is wonderful
every day
is a beautiful day
you were never born   you will never die

free from the human ghost
you & this island
will be just fine
no man is an island

precisely because he lacks
ecological integrity
trees birds sand & plants
waves & coral   beyond

human understanding
free from the human ghost
free from the distance
your painful body built for you

the wind makes a sound
the dove makes a sound
& you contribute your syllable
to an audible composition

mind the affectation
mind   pride of knowing &
choosing   you were so
very bright   & you remained

hidden from yourself
mind now stuck on one
syllable   ever
adventurous   you have gone

as far as you can
we wave from the shore
lord of sorrow
compels your simple song

what is that rumbling
i just heard
beside your balcony
coconuts up above ripen slowly

at the top of this palm tree
a local parrot rests briefly
on an extended branch
invisible beginner

you are becoming what is
next   though we
see you   & are with you
we cannot know

where & what you are
now   inhabitant
perhaps free
from habit   we

stare at a black box
you learn & feel
descent   back
to where you started from

to say the same same thing
is neither bitter nor sad
unless we say it's so
you make the sound

because you must
a neurological compulsion defiant
of science   the word you say
ma   ma   ma   is the same

inexplicable blankness we
see everywhere   perhaps it is
your return to a chosen
place   a ritual beyond

choice   at the wailing wall
within a world of perhaps
poem   or palm
at the end of mind

i am trying   4/19/2021
to become myself again this morning
& you it seems are entering
a quiet internal   some would say eternal

space   asleep instead of
shouting a repeated syllable
from your nurse we hear the term
metastatic cancer   & possible

cancer of the brain
& every path to death
is unpredictable   idiosyncratic
& all its own

no books   4/20/2021
no sops
no taters
no words

no mind
no place
no where
no how

no hope
no song
no sun
no nothing

trees stood green   4/21/2021
what did they mean
ma   ma   ma
said again & again

some hum a song
some sing it to
themselves   is there
something underneath

a painful climb
to the end of normal time
being so still
at the root of everything

AND THEN

1

to the one who died
      love goes by other names
            an invisible force

underneath each moment
      sits silently
            beside the one

who is trying to die
      does not judge
            does not question

opens up at the edge
      of presence
            in a temporary gown

mask & gloves
      listens to soothing music
            & reads rotating statements

the unanswered question
      what are you thinking
            what are you experiencing

there is no big story to tell
      no crashing dramatic moment
            only the slow enigmatic

enclosed present moment
      & minute fractal increments
            of your approach

to something
      we have designated as
            the end

we sit beside
      whatever is happening
            love

presence
       ignorance
             & limitation

intertwined
       we are held here
             beside you

a glimpse
       of the mystery
             all that our eyes can bear

2

why do we make the journey
   to these few words
      which of themselves

do not alter death & suffering
   in earlier years we sat
      in small groups listening to

& conjuring elusive explications
   free of that rigamarole
      we continue to return

would we really die for lack of
   what is said there
      where something sudden happens anyway

an impatient one said
        get to the point
                not knowing

that pointless itself
        is most true
                as we make

our appointed rounds
        who knew it would
                come to this

an old woman   eyes covered
        screaming from a comfortable
                bed   each

makes peace   or not
        with how it all
                turns out

step it up   step it down
        easeful as the passing days
                mercy   mercy makes us blind

to the fine increments of our aging
        reminded by the mirror
                & an aching lower back

no way then   even if you wanted it
        to be again   as you were
                wind on the balcony   clouds

across the mountain ridge
        & a meditative music
                refresh the beginning of the day

3

magpie or mockingbird
      what was it that i heard
            that so captured my hearing

& became for that moment
      a written music   not
            exactly knowing   no more

than ocean's sound on a sandy shore
      hear me out as i
            do the same

step by step
      measuring
            what is left

what sound was that
        this gray early morning day
                the story we tell

is one of will
        somehow she is we say
                hanging on

truly   will is not at play
        there is something else
                underneath

we just don't know
        & cannot say
                so turn to the also

confusing but visible
        world of our busy
                deeds & achievements

will it ever turn out
       as expected
              yes   sentences have a way

of reaching completion
       the old dog calls out
              for care & attention this

warm early morning
       messages pass back & forth
              conjecture & estimation

about an old woman who
       may or may not
              be dying   so many

words boil down to
       love &
              our helplessness

4

i sense there is an order
     other than chronology
          linking one thing

to another   for instance
     an event & a memory
          or the sudden demand

to be more specific   say
     strips of chicken breast
          black beans & rice

the old dog & the young one
     lying down together on
          one small gray bed

or where the mars helicopter *ingenuity*
     flies over a rocky plain
          named for octavia butler

or   untended at woods edge
          a small magnolia
                    is beginning to bloom

who among us has figured out
          what is our common need
                    if it's food shelter &

compassion   tell it to
          the cows pigs & chickens
                    thou shallt &

thou shallt not   but living
          happens more quickly than
                    thinking & intention

so someone gave us a gift
          four minutes & thirty-three seconds
                    of silence   to sit

& listen to this duration
      to be attentive to the particulars
          of being

is this not in fact our
      sacred common need
          turn away from it as we do

5

haste of words moves across
        the slowness of time
               one nurse says

you will die very soon
        another says stable & unchanged
               you gave me this gift

i present it to you
        why write a poem   such an
               unreasonable thing

because it is what i do
        a reckoning   a wreck
               beyond which there is no way you

can tell us what is next
        words press up to & fog the pane
               between us & it

empty form
      soon emptied of time
            we are wise to you

knowing there is no other way
      this impossible spring time
            where you live   an island in

perpetual bloom   tropical
      remembering too is such a bloom
            turned toward another light

suffering too is our communion
      we go down with you
            for there is no way out

being with you
      we are into it
            up to a point

dire & extreme
        without food or liquid
                you cannot move

though you move us
        in the screaming of your one syllable
                not rage   not disavowal

this enigma   just as anything
        resonant & suggestive
                of something else

as music sets a mood
        & is also
                simply itself

not in the service of some other
        purpose   your shoulders
                rise & fall with your breathing

i have it in good confidence
    that your pace maker
        will know to stop when you do

may you hear us speaking to you
    let us be with your breath
        that steady rise & fall

6

investigate & learn from
       what is immediate & near
              but what is that

is it what i see & touch
       or what i am
              thinking   is it

the invisible memory
       of sitting beside my mother's
              bed in her slow time

of dying   & what of this almost
       symmetrical cedar tree
              or the scent of a traditional

japanese incense   or wet dogs
       at rest after their early
              morning run

maybe it's the taste of coffee or
        a white pickup truck
                rumbling along the gravel road

you took great pleasure in beautiful music
        fine food (without garlic!)
                & expensive jewelry & handbags

good coffee   certain cheeses for
        your morning cheese toast
                but none of this

gets to the heart of the matter
        & these acquisitions
                are not why i will miss you

your death marks the end
        of a living connection to
                early Brooklyn &

before that life   family stories
        of Russia & the dangerous
                path to America

the last six weeks of your life
were such a terror
that at your death

i felt mostly relief
having seen you trapped
in that bed wanting to die

but unable to
reduced to a body with closed eyes
& open hearing

able to say one syllable   *MA   MA   MA*
again & again
we assumed you sensed

our presence
but there was no way to know
what was going on inside

painful to sit & witness
because you had always been
so articulate

for better or for worse
      i carry forward elements
            of your nature

as i prepare my morning coffee
      read the news   & enter into
           the day's writing

7

the postal package arrived
      $74.85 postage & a big label
            CREMATED REMAINS

is this what & where
      you are   there is no "I"
          & yet there was one

an embodiment released from pain
      to circulate in stories in pictures
          in jewelry (i wear your jade necklace)

in the invisible & personal rituals
      of a son & daughter
          inventing their own ways of grieving

love & compassion
      saturated
          in a time of not knowing

the sustaining mystery
        of breath
                comes to an end

your death
        becomes the foretaste
                of our own

i wonder   really
        who cares about the death
                of someone else's mother

unless each death
        is every death
                & then there is

the confusing erratic
        pathway that grieving
                relief & remembrance

take
        in the weeks following
                her death

slow knowledge of her
       physical absence
              the disappearance

of a voice & its
       peculiarities & repetitions
              her desk   her possessions

her kindle   her iPad   her pens
       her special lighting
              the difficult synchronization

of all her devices
       the closets full of clothes
              the books   the paintings

the knickknacks
       the coffee cups
              her wishes about what

should happen after her death
       all of this a bundle
              set against the depth

of her absence
       the living
              no matter how loving

are predatory & distracted
       moving away from the black hole
              of your disappearance

ashes in a box
       the weight of your remains
              rings & necklaces

am i
       what is left
              of your body

to say i taste
       your death in
              my morning coffee

tells me your death
       is interwoven into
              my own days & years

along a possible pathway
for my own
& every dying

ABOUT THE AUTHOR

HANK LAZER has published thirty-three books of poetry, including *field recordings of mind in morning* (2021, BlazeVOX – with 15 music-poetry tracks with Holland Hopson on banjo – available from Bandcamp), *COVID 19 SUTRAS* (2020, Lavender Ink), *Slowly Becoming Awake (N32)* (2019, Dos Madres Press), *Poems That Look Just Like Poems* (2019, PURH – one volume in English, one in French), *Evidence of Being Here: Beginning in Havana (N27)*, (2018, Negative Capability Press), *Thinking in Jewish (N20)* (2017, Lavender Ink). Lazer has performed jazz-poetry improvisations in the US and Cuba with musicians Davey Williams, Omar Pérez, Andrew Raffo Dewar, Holland Hopson, and others. Lazer's *Brush Mind* books have been transformed into video installations and performances in several art gallery venues. In 2015, Lazer received Alabama's most prestigious literary prize, the Harper Lee Award, for lifetime achievement in literature. Lazer has been quarantining in Tuscaloosa, Alabama, and at Duncan Farm in Carrollton, Alabama. To order books, learn about talks, readings, and workshops, and see photos of Duncan Farm see Lazer's website: https://www.hanklazer.com

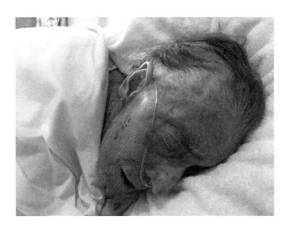

Other books by Hank Lazer
published by Dos Madres Press

Slowly Becoming Awake (N32) (2019)

For the full Dos Madres Press catalog:
www.dosmadres.com